Giving It to You Real: What You Need to Know about College that Your Advisor Doesn't Tell You

Giving It to You Real: What You Need to Know about College that Your Advisor Doesn't Tell You

By

Amanda S. Quashie Blackman

Visit us at: www.impressivelyyou.com

Publisher contact information:

impressivelyu@gmail.com

Printed in the United States of America

ISBN # 978-0-578-44764-3

I wish you the best in all your future endeavors

Acknowledgments

This book would not have been possible without the many people that provided support, patience, encouragement, and feedback so I would be able to publish a piece that will create a positive impact on the lives of other students.

To my lovely parents, Julie and Lee, and my beautiful sisters, Allysha and Avlyn, thank you!

I would like to thank my close friends, college peers, church family, and coworkers for continuing to motivate me throughout the process of writing the book.

Thank you to Dr. M. Christian, Dominique, and the faculty of the Africana Studies Department, who are more like aunties and uncles to me. Every one of you has made a positive impact on my life, and I thank you all for that.

A special thanks to my SEEK and TRiO family for being a great support system throughout my years at Lehman College, even after having graduated.

Lastly, forgive me for those whose names I have not mentioned, who have been with me especially throughout my college journey. Thank you!

Table of Contents

A Letter to You

Hey there!

I'm sure when you read the title of this book, you knew it was the answer to your academic trials and tribulations. I am happy that I can be of help to you in the midst of it all. At a time when you're preparing to go off to college or maybe you're already in college and are struggling to declare your major, you may still be a bit skeptical of what career you would like to pursue. Now, you're probably wondering why you should trust this book. Well, just like you, I was an undergraduate student stuck in the same situation. I've realized that when it comes to education, it isn't the work that drags you down, it's the lack of time. It seems like we do not have enough of it. In the case of seeking advice on what colleges to attend or what major to declare, you often have to wait and make an appointment to meet with a college advisor or guidance counselor. However, we all have other responsibilities outside of school, such as work or duties given to us by our parents, kids, etc. So I wrote this book to be a guide that you can take everywhere, to assist you with what major to declare and which career path to follow, and overall, to give you some educational advice and support, so you can feel confident making the best choices for you.

Your new friend,

Amanda

Persistence

One of the most important things you can do as a high school senior is to be persistent and stay on top of things with your guidance counselor; he/she is crucial to your college planning process. Yes, your guidance counselor might get annoyed with you constantly knocking on their door to ask about your college applications, recommendations, etc. However, this is your future we're talking about here! You must also keep in mind that you are not the only student your guidance counselor has to take care of, so they might forget things sometimes. It may not be that your guidance counselor is disorganized; he or she must wear multiple caps, including being a guidance counselor first, along with being a college-readiness advisor. Aside from just focusing on a students' educational and social growth, a guidance counselor must also focus on the students' overall well-being. According to the American School Counselor Association (ASCA), "ASCA's recommended student-to-school counselor ratio is 250 to 1" (Bray, 2017, para. 5). However, this is not the case in many states, which may have a student-to-school counselor ratio of about 400:1 or even higher. If this is the case for your school, you especially need to be responsible throughout your senior year.

Story Time

Towards the ending of tenth grade, I transferred from one school to another to complete the rest of my high school career. When I officially started my senior year of high school, the senior students had to meet with our guidance counselor to see if we were on track to graduate, and supposedly I wasn't. My Living Environment Lab was missing from my transcript, even though I had taken the class and the Regents (statewide standardized examination) for it. When I transferred out of the previous school everything on my transcript seemed to be fine, but I didn't notice that the Living Environment Lab was missing on it. Once we figured out what the issue was, my guidance counselor called my former school, and they agreed they would fix the issue.

At least a month prior to graduation, my guidance counselor did a double check again, and he still hadn't received a transcript with the corrections. Now, my guidance counselor was organized, but unfortunately, he was the only guidance counselor for grades nine through twelve. Luckily for me, I have a persistent mother who takes her children's education seriously. My mother and I called my previous school, my former principal rectified the issue, and I was able to pick up my updated transcript the same day. Long story short, I was able to graduate with my senior class. The moral of the story is, don't wait around for someone to get something done for you that you can try to get done for yourself. Remember that persistence is key.

Community Colleges and Four-Year Institutions

This chapter is one of my favorite topics of discussion, because I believe students often do not desire to start their college careers at a community college due to stigmas about them. Some students believe that they aren't able to have an authentic college life experience at a community college, that it isn't "real college," etc. One reason there is a stigma about attending a community college is that many community colleges may not be as selective as four-year institutions; most of them have open admissions (the student is eligible for admission as long as they graduated from high school or have a GED). Although the community college itself may not be selective, keep in mind that there may be programs at the school that are selective, such as nursing, engineering, those that you have to audition for, etc. These programs may have specific admission conditions, and require a separate application in addition to the general admission application to get into the school.

When you are considering your options for college, don't rule out community colleges. There is nothing wrong with starting off at a community college, and there are many benefits. Although most students would rather go straight into four-year institutions, some may not have that option available at first. If that is the case for you, it is good to understand that you will have the opportunity to transfer to another school after completing your associate's degree. You may even be able to transfer schools before finishing your associate's if you're able to meet the admission requirements for a four-year institution. Keep in mind that it's not how you start, but how you finish. If you were only accepted to a community college, do not despair. Continue to push yourself to accomplish what you initially sought for yourself.

Note: Community colleges have tuition rates which are less than those of four-year institutions. Sometimes students that meet the admission requirements for a four-year institution attend a community college first because they have a lower tuition rate.

Making Good Financial Decisions for College

As I worked in the admissions office during my undergraduate career, there were often hectic days. However, those hectic days didn't stop me from enjoying the job. When I wasn't answering phone calls, I had the pleasure of assisting with and facilitating information sessions, leading college tours, representing my school in recruitment events, etc. During those moments, I felt that aside from being an employee, I was able to be an influential student and sprinkle a bit of knowledge onto others, particularly high schoolers getting ready to go off to college. Most times high school students would tell me that they would prefer to go away for college because of their interest in moving to a new atmosphere, to get away from their "annoying" parents, or for other personal reasons. In turn, I would use that as an opportunity to bring up the financial aspect of college. Usually, the conversations would go in depth, with many students coming to the conclusion that they wouldn't be able to afford to go away for college. I would then proceed to explain to them how to get funding for college through financial aid, which includes grants, scholarships, work study, etc. Students can normally find these opportunities by referring to their guidance counselors or college scholarship/financial aid offices, or through scholarship websites. As a person that was also learning to make good financial decisions, I knew that sinking in loads of debt is not where I planned to be. So when deciding on what college to attend, be sure to compare each school's estimated college costs (including tuition and fees, room and board, books and supplies, personal expenses, and transportation) and/or the financial-aid packages that you are offered by each school.

Note: There are different student loan forgiveness options to choose from if you take out a loan, you are also not guaranteed approval for loan forgiveness. Some examples are getting a public service or government job, serving in the military, or even teaching in a low-income-neighborhood public school. However, if you can avoid taking out a loan, then take the opportunity not to be in debt starting as an undergrad.

Note: Aside from the financial aspect when deciding on which college to attend, also read each institutions website thoroughly, visit the school, look at their graduation rate and what support services are offered, especially for first-generation and low-income students.

Transitioning from High School to College

Learning to adapt to a new environment is imperative to the transition from being a high schooler to being a college student. This new adaptation, of course, may be somewhat difficult for college freshmen at first, but it'll become easier once you are accustomed to it. During the summer, prior to the start of my freshman year of college, I made sure to know the campus like the back of my hand, the routes I could take to get to school since I commuted from home, and what academic resources were available in case I needed help.

It is important to remember that in college, no one is going to run behind you to see if you completed your work. College, in a sense, is like survival of the fittest: it's every man for themselves in the hunt toward a degree.

Also, do not adopt the habit of comparing yourself to other classmates or colleagues. It is important to have tunnel vision and focus on yourself and your journey.

Story Time

During my first semester of college, I thought I wasn't going to do well in one of my classes because I struggled to excel on the quizzes. In this same class, there was a group of girls that always sat in the front of the room that did well on their quizzes. Focusing on how well others were doing on their quizzes caused me to lose focus of my own tunnel vision and forget about other things that mattered. It made me overlook the fact that I consistently participated in class, completed my homework on time, and made sure my attendance was on point. Most importantly, I forgot all about the syllabus which stated that quizzes were not worth a very large percentage of the class grade; the end-of-term project and term paper were worth the majority of the grade. And guess what? When the end of the semester came around, I got an A in the class! From that first semester onward, I focused more on what *I* was doing and did not concern myself with other people who seemed to be doing better than me. I learned that may not always be the case, as some of those girls who sat in the front did not pass the class. Another thing to take note of is that the syllabus you get in every class is your best friend throughout your college career. Please also note that each professor you take will operate their classes differently than the next, so don't think that everything is going to be the same for each class. For example, if you miss an assignment for one professor without a valid excuse, such as going to a doctor's appointment, you might get lucky and they will allow you to make it up. However, another professor might say no, especially if the excuse is not valid. Overall, just mind your P's and Q's. It is okay to make mistakes, but just make sure to learn from them so you don't repeat them again. College, after all, is supposed to be a learning experience.

Surviving Undergrad

Some students probably buy many college survival guides and forget most of what they read. To make it easy for you, I've decided to come up with a few simple survival tips to help you create your own college experience without feeling overwhelmed.

1. READ, READ, READ! Make sure you pay attention in class, check your personal email/school email daily, and read everything your professors give you thoroughly, especially the syllabus they give you at the beginning of the semester.

2. Become a better listener or an active listener. This may be hard at times, especially if you have something important you want to say and you want to say it before you forget, which is understandable. By being an active listener, you will be able to understand what people are saying when they speak to you.

3. Before your first semester starts, get a tour of the campus, so you know where your classes are located. This is much better than waiting until the first day and ending up spending five or ten minutes trying to locate one class.

4. Create a classmate buddy system by exchanging phone numbers with at least two or more classmates from each of your classes. By doing

this you can be each other's back up for missed class information in the case that you couldn't attend a class.

5. Utilize your professors' office hours. Even if you don't have an initial reason to go talk with your professor, create a reason to go. This is an opportunity for you to get to know your professors and ask for help when needed. If you are a consistent office-hour visitor, they will get to know you and remember you, especially if you stand out to them. Trust me, this is a future recommendation waiting to happen (think of graduate school or references for future jobs).

6. Don't wait until the last minute to ask for help. If you know you're struggling in a class, don't wait until around midterms to try to get it together, because once midterms hit, you know that the end of the semester is near. If you wait until the last minute to ask professors for help, that doesn't look too good. And you shouldn't expect professors to come to you. After all, it is your grade, not your professors'.

7. Meet with your academic advisor at the beginning and end of each semester. (Meeting with an academic advisor may be mandatory at some institutions). By meeting with your academic advisor, you can update them on what changes you would like to make to your

academic plan or career path, so they can better assist you going forward.

8. Do internships, volunteer, study abroad, or even do an independent research study. This is a great way to gain experience for your future career while in college, instead of waiting until you graduate to gain experience. These are also great things to add to your resume that'll make it stand out more.

9. Meet with a career advisor to help you update your resume when needed, talk about internships and jobs, or even help you master the skills needed to ace your interviews.

10. Again, mingle, mingle, mingle. Join student organizations or clubs; get involved. By doing so you can develop relationships with individuals who you can refer back to in the future (perhaps a future business relationship) and who can also help you along the way to achieving your academic and career goals.

11. Learn to manage your time well. Time and I are not the best of friends, because it goes by so fast, especially when I'm not looking. Stay on top of your time management by keeping track of deadlines. If you must, buy a planner, put alarms for deadlines on the calendar in your phone, or put reminders on sticky notes and attach them to

the inside of your laptop, so when you open your laptop, you will see them.

12. Don't procrastinate. We all procrastinate sometimes, but that is not to say that you should. Some people can work well under pressure, but for most of us, procrastination only leads to being overwhelmed and performing poorly.

13. Download college apps that can help you throughout your college career, so you can be that studious and organized student.

14. Practice self-care. Don't forget that you have only one life, so take care of your well-being, mentally, socially, physically, and spiritually. For instance, Sunday is basically my self-care day. On those days I give myself an at-home spa day, do my meal preps, and try to get myself ready to start a brand-new week.

What If I Don't Know What to Major In?

****If you do know what to major in, you can skip to the next chapter****

I understand that you don't know what to major in, but please try not to stress out about it. You'll figure it out. Aside from my passion for the education field, I've always had a passion for the healthcare field too. When I was younger I didn't know that there were so many careers that can lead to working in healthcare. When I did some more research, I was so excited. I did not have to be a physician, surgeon, etc. to work in a healthcare setting; I could do the complete opposite. The complete opposite, of course, involved using my strengths to my advantage, and so should you!

Note: If there is an area you are interested in but may still be skeptical about because you have a lot of other options in mind, consider taking courses, volunteering, or do an internship in that area.

The following are the steps I took to decide what I wanted to major in, along with the exercises I did to help me decide. After I go through each of my examples, I have provided space so you can write down your answers and start to gain clarity about your major.

My Example: STEP 1

List the subject areas that are your strengths and those that need improvement:

Strengths	Need Improvement
English	Pure mathematics (E.g., physics, calc.)
History	
Business	

<h2 align="center">Your Turn: STEP 1</h2>

List the subject areas that are your strengths and those that need improvement:

Strengths	Need Improvement

My Example: STEP 2

Since I already knew what my strengths were and that I wanted to work in healthcare, I checked out the majors in my school's Health Sciences Department and picked the ones that sparked my interest.

This is pretty easy to do. Just use the internet to visit your school's website and look up the academic department's or major's listing.

Majors I Am Interested In:

1) Physical Therapy/Exercise Science

2) Health Education and Promotion

3) Therapeutic Recreation

4) Health Services Administration

5) Recreation Education

Your Turn: STEP 2

List the majors you're interested in:

STEP 3

If your school doesn't have the course listings and descriptions of the majors on the website, visit the department and ask for a pamphlet or paper with information for each major on it. If your school has the information online, skip to Step 4.

STEP 4

When I looked through the descriptions and the course outlines of each major thoroughly, I narrowed my results down to two majors. They were as follows:

1) Health Education and Promotion
2) Health Services Administration

Your Turn: Step 4

Narrow your results down to two possible majors.

STEP 5

To get some more information on the majors I chose in Step 4, I also visited one of my favorite websites, **www.bigfuture.org**.

STEP 6

After looking up the two majors on the website, I read the information thoroughly for both of them. Then I decided that the Health Services Administration major would be a better fit, especially since it fit the description of what I was looking for: business specifically for the healthcare field.

Your Turn: Step 6

Decide which of the two majors you have narrowed down is a better fit for

what you want to do in a career.

STEP 7

Lastly, follow the steps from the "What If I Know What to Major In?" chapter.

Tip #1:

You should still meet with your academic advisor to make sure you are fully on track to graduate. You should meet with them twice per semester (once at the beginning and once at the end).

Tip #2:

Being curious, by taking different courses than those you think you are interested in or that don't spark your interest at first glance, can lead you to decide on a major.

What If I Know What to Major In?

In this chapter, I will show you the vital steps I took to declare my major and how I stuck to my decision. In the early stages of our educational journey, our teachers often asked us, "What do you want to be when you grow up?" The most common answers were a doctor, a lawyer, a police officer, a firefighter, a nurse, etc. Of course, when I got older I came to realize that there are lots of careers, some that I've never even heard of before. I actually had this huge panned-out idea in my head since high school, that I would become an occupational therapist and open up my own practice. However, when I started college I realized that wasn't the path for me. It is important to remember that even though you might know what you want to major in now, that can change at any time. Since you already know what you want to major in, on the following pages is a simple four-step process to make sure you are headed in the right direction and on track to getting the degree you want.

STEP 1

If you already know what you want to major in, the next step is to declare your major and talk with your major advisor about what classes you should enroll in.

STEP 2

After the advising session is done, make sure you ask the major advisor for a pamphlet or course outline for the major. This can help you be organized and know what classes you have to enroll in each following semester.

STEP 3

If you attend a school where you have two advisors (a general academic advisor and a major advisor), be sure to update your general academic advisor on the major that you chose if you did not do so already. This is another way of making sure all your ducks are in a row.

Different Majors That Lead into the Same Career

Did you know that there are different majors that can lead to the same career? If you didn't know, maybe this example I am going to give can help shed some light. Ideally, a student that wants to be a social worker would major in social work during their undergraduate studies. But say, for instance, the school doesn't offer social work as a major. The student can then do some research or ask a career advisor at their school about what types of majors can lead to the same career. Based on this social work major example, psychology or sociology can be another option that the student can look into. If a student is majoring in psychology or sociology and they plan to continue on and get their master's in social work (which they should), they should note that each educational institution has their own requirements. With some programs, if a student did not initially receive a bachelor's degree in social work, the student may be admissible for a traditional MSW program (typically completed in two years) instead of an advanced/accelerated MSW program (completed in one year). If you happen to find yourself in a similar situation where your school does not offer your degree of interest, just do some research on what other majors can lead you to your intended career choice or consider transferring to a different school that offers your program choice.

Note: Aside from different majors leading to the same career, there are also majors that are worded differently that could also mean the same

thing such as: health services administration, healthcare management, healthcare administration.

Making a Career Decision

Throughout my time working in college admissions and being a student, I've come to realize that prior to college some students are stuck in a trance. What I mean by this is that they have envisioned who they want to be in the future, but they struggle to make preparations to achieve their career goals. I'm not saying to throw in the towel or give up, but perhaps by taking a different approach, you can achieve the same goals. Keep in mind your weaknesses do not determine your intelligence; you also have strengths—use them to your advantage. One of the subject areas I needed to put extra effort into was math, but that doesn't mean that I don't know how to count, or can't take math classes and do very well in them. It just means that I'm not going to set myself up for failure by majoring in mathematics, or anything of the sort. Another thing that I have seen a couple of times is one friend choosing to go into a career field because another friend is. I can recall two girls who were best friends since high school that chose to go to the same college and major in nursing. At the end of their freshman year, one of them had successfully passed her prerequisite classes, while the other was not so successful. When she told me that she didn't know what to do, I asked her if nursing is what she really wanted to do. Her response was, "I don't know." Since she didn't know if she wanted to go into nursing or not, I suggested that she take a look at all of the majors being offered at her school and not fully abandon the idea of nursing school just yet. Overall, the moral of the story is, just because one person does something and receives certain results doesn't mean that you will receive the same results.

In the next few pages, I will go in-depth on what steps you can take in choosing your career path. Stay tuned.

STEP 1

Make a list of things you are interested in and passionate about:

E.g.: art, education, etc.

STEP 2

Search for a career assessment test online, take the test, and look at the results. As you look through the results, highlight or write down the careers you think you might be interested in. After you have made your list of the careers you might be interested in, research each of them (use the websites listed below to also help you) and ask professors or professionals working in the field questions about the careers you have in mind. When you have finished your research, narrow down the jobs/careers list again by picking the ones you are really interested in.

www.bls.gov

www.bigfuture.org

Note: The Bureau of Labor Statistics (BLS) is a great source to turn to when trying to find out information about various careers. The BLS provides statistical information about changes in wages, employment, and unemployment and can even give you an outlook of how much demand there will be for your future career in the years to come.

STEP 3

Make a list of skills and qualities you have and need to work on:

E.g.: Microsoft Office Suite, interpersonal skills, public speaking, etc.

Skills I Have Right Now	Skills I Need to Work On

STEP 4

Using the narrowed-down list of jobs or careers that you came up with after you completed the research on each of them, match your skills, qualities, and strengths you have in certain academic areas with the jobs.

STEP 5

Do an internship or volunteer. Some people would rather have a paid internship, but that should not be your focus. Your focus should be on gaining the necessary experience to get a start in the career you have envisioned yourself being in, or maybe just to get a feel for a career before you make your final decision on which career you really want.

Warning #1

Do not make your decisions based on the hopes and plans your parents, friends, or family has for you. This is your life, and you only have one to live, so don't base your decisions on what other people think. You need to start making your own decisions, especially in areas that will have a huge impact on your life.

Warning #2

Try not to make any decisions based solely on money. However, make sure that the decision you make won't leave you broke. Do something you love or you're passionate about, while also making sure that you're financially stable.

Network = Net Worth

"Mingle, mingle, mingle" is a phrase I often find myself repeating over and over again to my peers. This is because throughout my undergraduate experience, I've learned that college offers more than academics; it is also where you establish and create your network empire. Networking is simply building relationships with others. Your network empire grows as you encounter and connect with new people, which also exposes you to more opportunities that will help you advance your career. Honestly, it doesn't matter if you go to a commuter school, where you travel back and forth between home and school every day, or you go away to school, where you live on campus. I have to say this because sometimes I run into students who attend commuter schools and they are always in a rush to go home right after class. By the time they get to their senior year, they find themselves struggling to get recommendations for graduate school. The reason for this is they never thought about the importance of getting involved with extracurricular activities, networking, and meeting new people who possibly could be their link to recommendation letters. Like, c'mon, get involved! As a student who went to a commuter school, I developed a mindset of getting all of my schoolwork done before going home.

Aside from my schoolwork, I managed to join a couple of student organizations during my freshman year of college as well. One, in particular, was the African Students Association (ASA). Determined to grow my network, I made sure to attend the majority of their events. At the end of my freshman year, I was able to attain a position on the ASA executive board as president. During my three-year presidency, the African Students Association adopted the new name: the African & Caribbean Students Association. Throughout those years my executive board and I were invited to events off campus, where we were able to meet other student leaders like ourselves, as well as professionals from various industries. Aside from attending off-campus events, we also hosted our own events on campus. One event, in particular, was our annual networking event at the beginning of each academic school year, which we hosted by using the concept of speed dating. The speed-dating mixer was a fun way to get our peers not only to interact with each other, but also to build their network. As you continue on your college journey, remember to mingle, connect, and make conscious efforts in establishing your network empire.

Tip: Look up free or affordable networking events on campus or in the area where you live.

College Is Not for Me

At the beginning of this book, I wrote a letter pertaining to you knowing yourself better than anyone else. The purpose of that letter is, being that you know yourself and the goals you have set best, it makes it easier to decide what you want to do in the future. Whether you've never gone to college, or started and put it on hold, don't give up hope if you've realized that it isn't for you. There is also the option of choosing to go through certificate programs, such as those for medical assistants, licensed practical nurses, electricians, mechanical engineering technicians, construction workers, plumbers, etc. If you believe college isn't for you, try looking for a vocational school. There are many vocational schools to choose from, but be sure to get your money's worth, especially if you're paying out of pocket. There are also tuition-free vocational programs available out there if you take the time to look. In addition, research vocational schools in your city that have various programs to choose from and have great success reviews. Furthermore, you can even try doing an apprenticeship. By doing an apprenticeship, you can work full time while being trained and paid.

Just keep in mind that as time goes by, job requirements pertaining to educational backgrounds can change. Also remember that many people go back to school later in life for various reasons: some for a career change, some to finish college that they started years ago, and some because of new job expectations. So don't fully abandon the idea of college; it could still be an option for you in the future.

Y.E.P (Yearly Educational Planner)

I suggest having a yearly educational planner (Y.E.P) for the length of your college career. The purpose of a YEP is to help keep you organized throughout your academic semesters, so you are on track to graduate. I have filled one out as an example below, and then I have included blanks after that for you to use each semester.

YEP Example

****Don't forget to put how many credits each course is worth. Also, at the end of each semester, insert the grade you received next to each class****

Fall 2018		Winter 2018
1) HSA 431 (3 credits)	A	1)
2) HSA 432 (3 credits)	A	2)
3) HSA 433 (3 credits)	A	3)
4)		4)
5)		5)
6)		6)
Total Credits: 9 **Cum GPA: 4.0**		**Total Credits:** **Cum GPA:**

Spring 2018	Summer 2018
1)	1)
2)	2)
3)	3)
4)	4)
5)	5)
6)	6)
Total Credits: **Cum GPA:**	**Total Credits:** **Cum GPA:**

Notes:

YEP (Yearly Educational Planner)

Year #1: Freshman

Fall	Winter
1)	1)
2)	2)
3)	3)
4)	4)
5)	5)
6)	6)
Total Credits: Cum GPA:	Total Credits: Cum GPA:

Spring	Summer
1)	1)
2)	2)
3)	3)
4)	4)
5)	5)
6)	6)
Total Credits: Cum GPA:	Total Credits: Cum GPA:

Notes:

Year #2: Sophomore

Fall	Winter
1)	1)
2)	2)
3)	3)
4)	4)
5)	5)
6)	6)
Total Credits: Cum GPA:	Total Credits: Cum GPA:

Spring	Summer
1)	1)
2)	2)
3)	3)
4)	4)
5)	5)
6)	6)
Total Credits: Cum GPA:	Total Credits: Cum GPA:

Notes:

Year #3: Junior

Fall	Winter
1)	1)
2)	2)
3)	3)
4)	4)
5)	5)
6)	6)
Total Credits: Cum GPA:	Total Credits: Cum GPA:

Spring	Summer
1)	1)
2)	2)
3)	3)
4)	4)
5)	5)
6)	6)
Total Credits: Cum GPA:	Total Credits: Cum GPA:

Notes:

Year #4: Graduating!

Fall	Winter
1)	1)
2)	2)
3)	3)
4)	4)
5)	5)
6)	6)
Total Credits: Cum GPA:	Total Credits: Cum GPA:

Spring	Summer
1)	1)
2)	2)
3)	3)
4)	4)
5)	5)
6)	6)
Total Credits: Cum GPA:	Total Credits: Cum GPA:

Notes:

Year #5: Just in Case You Needed an Extra Year – Graduating!

Fall	Winter
1)	1)
2)	2)
3)	3)
4)	4)
5)	5)
6)	6)
Total Credits: Cum GPA:	Total Credits: Cum GPA:

Spring	Summer
1)	1)
2)	2)
3)	3)
4)	4)
5)	5)
6)	6)
Total Credits: Cum GPA:	Total Credits: Cum GPA:

Notes:

Epilogue

Now that you have finished reading this book you are even closer to achieving your academic or career goal(s). It's up to you now to implement what you have learned. Just remember that we can never get time back, so do what you can starting today, and make things happen!

You got this!

Author Contact Information

E-mail: impressivelyu@gmail.com

Website: www.impressivelyyou.com

References

Bray, B. (2017, October 24). U.S. student-to-school counselor ratio shows slight improvement. Retrieved January 7, 2018, from http://ct.counseling.org/2017/10/u-s-student-school-counselor-ratio-shows-slight-improvement/

U.S. Bureau of Labor Statistics. (n.d.). Retrieved January 7, 2018, from http://www.bls.gov/

Find the right college for you. (n.d.). Retrieved January 7, 2018, from http://www.bigfuture.org/

<u>NOTES</u>